Rookie Read-About™ Science

Woolly Sheep and Hungry Goats

By Allan Fow

Consultants:

Robert L. Hillerich, Ph.D., Bowling Green
State University, Bowling Green, Ohio

Mary Nalbandian, Director of Science,
Chicago Public Schools, Chicago, Illinois

Fay Robinson, Child Development Specialist

CHILDRENS PRESS®

CHICAGO

Design by Beth Herman Design Associates

Library of Congress Cataloging-in-Publication Data

Fowler, Allan
    Woolly sheep and hungry goats / by Allan Fowler.
      p. cm. –(Rookie read-about science)
    Summary: Provides general information about sheep and goats and
some of the products, such as cheese and wool, that we get from them.
    ISBN 0-516-06014-7
    1. Sheep–Juvenile literature. 2. Goats–Juvenile literature.
    [1. Sheep. 2. Goats.] I. Title. II. Series: Fowler, Allan. Rookie read-
about science.
SF375.2.F69 1993
636.3–dc20   92-36366
                                                CIP
                                                AC

Did you know that there are wild sheep and goats in the Rocky Mountains?

These bighorn sheep and
Rocky Mountain goats
can climb steep mountains
without slipping.

But most goats and sheep
are found on farms or
ranches.

A male sheep is a ram.
He has big, curly horns.

A female sheep is a ewe –
sounds like "you." Many
ewes have no horns.

Their babies, called lambs, love to play and run and jump.

Sheep spend their days
grazing – eating grass –
in the pasture.

The person who takes care
of sheep is called a shepherd.

He is helped by a smart dog.

Sometimes a lamb wanders off from the flock.

The dog chases it back before it gets lost.

Some kinds of sheep, such as merinos, are raised for their wool.

Other kinds of sheep are raised for meat.

A sheep's thick coat of
wool never stops growing.

Every spring the wool
is cut off, or sheared,
like this.

Don't worry – this doesn't
hurt the sheep.

In fact, if the man didn't shear her, she'd be too hot in the summer.

The wool is made into yarn, which is made into suits and dresses, sweaters, and coats –

so you won't be too cold
in the winter.

We also get wool, such
as fine angora, from
certain kinds of goats.

Goat's milk is good for
drinking and making cheese.

A goat eats any kind of plant – grass, fruit, leaves, vegetables, even tree bark.

Both males, called billy
goats, and females, called
nanny goats, have horns.

But goats on farms usually
have their horns removed.
This is so goats don't hurt
each other or get their
horns caught in fences.

Only billy goats have beards.

People can be like sheep
or goats in certain ways.

A person who is ashamed
or embarrassed is said to
be "sheepish."

A very playful person
is said to be "as frisky
as a lamb."

A man's beard that looks
like a goat's beard is called
a goatee.

And children are called kids
– the same as baby goats.
No kidding.

Words You Know

sheep   grazing   pasture

ram   horns   ewe   lamb

billy goat   nanny goat   kids

shepherd   flock

shear   merinos   wool

Index

About the Author

Allan Fowler is a free-lance writer with a background in advertising. Born in New York, he lives in Chicago now and enjoys traveling.

Photo Credits

Animals Animals – ©Adrienne T. Gibson, 14, 31 (bottom right); ©John L. Pontier, 22

PhotoEdit – ©Alan Oddie, 6, 23, 30 (bottom left); ©David Young-Wolff, 19; ©Myrleen Ferguson, 27

SuperStock International, Inc. – ©R. Smith, 5; ©Schuster, 7, 30 (bottom right); ©VanHoorick, 9, 30 (top); ©Conrad Sims, 11 (center right); ©E. Carle, 15; ©BL Productions, 17, 31 (bottom left); ©T. Rosenthal, 24, 31 (top right); ©Kris Coppieters, 31 (center right)

Valan – ©J.A. Wilkinson, Cover; ©Wayne Lankinen, 4 (left); ©Val & Alan Wilkinson, 8; ©Phil Norton, 20; ©Kennon Cooke, 28

Visuals Unlimited – ©Ron Spomer, 4 (right); ©LINK, 12; ©William J. Weber, 21, 27 (inset); ©Gustav Verderber, 25, 31 (top left); ©John D. Cunningham, 29

Cover: Sheep and goats at a petting zoo